IT'S TIME TO EAT MUSTARD GREENS

It's Time to Eat MUSTARD GREENS

Walter the Educator

Silent King Books
A WhichHead Entertainment Imprint

Copyright © 2025 by Walter the Educator

All rights reserved. No part of this book may be reproduced in any manner whatsoever without written per- mission except in the case of brief quotations embodied in critical articles and reviews.

First Printing, 2024

Disclaimer

This book is a literary work; the story is not about specific persons, locations, situations, and/or circumstances unless mentioned in a historical context. Any resemblance to real persons, locations, situations, and/or circumstances is coincidental. This book is for entertainment and informational purposes only. The author and publisher offer this information without warranties expressed or implied. No matter the grounds, neither the author nor the publisher will be accountable for any losses, injuries, or other damages caused by the reader's use of this book. The use of this book acknowledges an understanding and acceptance of this disclaimer.

It's Time to Eat MUSTARD GREENS is a collectible early learning book by Walter the Educator suitable for all ages belonging to Walter the Educator's Time to Eat Book Series. Collect more books at WaltertheEducator.com

USE THE EXTRA SPACE TO TAKE NOTES AND DOCUMENT YOUR MEMORIES

MUSTARD GREENS

It's time to eat, come take a seat,

It's Time to Eat
Mustard Greens

A yummy meal that's fresh and neat!

Something green is on my plate,

I take a bite, I just can't wait!

These leafy greens are bright and bold,

A little spicy, fresh, not cold.

They're mustard greens, so fun to eat,

A tasty, healthy, crunchy treat!

Cook them soft or eat them raw,

Either way, they make me go, "Aww!"

With garlic, onions, lemon too,

They make a super tasty stew!

Grandma stirs them in a pot,

She says, "They're good and help a lot!"

Full of goodness, strong they make,

A bite is all you need to take!

It's Time to Eat
Mustard Greens

Dip them in a sauce so sweet,

Or mix them up with rice and meat.

Crunchy, tender, full of cheer,

They bring good health all through the year!

Brother says, "I'll give them a try,"

He chews and says, "Oh my, oh my!"

"They taste so fresh, just like a breeze,

I think I'll have some more of these!"

Sister takes a little bite,

She grins and says, "This tastes just right!"

Mom and Dad both smile with glee,

We love mustard greens, you see!

Big and leafy, soft and bright,

They help our tummies feel so light.

With vitamins to help us grow,

It's Time to Eat
Mustard Greens

They're good for me, this much I know!

So when it's time to eat again,

Mustard greens will be my friend!

With every bite, I feel so strong,

Eating greens can't go wrong!

Now our meal is all but done,

Eating greens was so much fun!

Thank you, greens, so bright and bold,

It's Time to Eat Mustard Greens

For making us healthy, strong, and bold!

ABOUT THE CREATOR

Walter the Educator is one of the pseudonyms for Walter Anderson. Formally educated in Chemistry, Business, and Education, he is an educator, an author, a diverse entrepreneur, and he is the son of a disabled war veteran. "Walter the Educator" shares his time between educating and creating. He holds interests and owns several creative projects that entertain, enlighten, enhance, and educate, hoping to inspire and motivate you. Follow, find new works, and stay up to date with Walter the Educator™

at WaltertheEducator.com

www.ingramcontent.com/pod-product-compliance
Lightning Source LLC
LaVergne TN
LVHW052013060526
838201LV00059B/4013